LINCOLNSHIRE RAILWAYS

PATRICK BENNETT

AMBERLEY

First published 2021

Amberley Publishing
The Hill, Stroud
Gloucestershire, GL5 4EP

www.amberley-books.com

Copyright © Patrick Bennett, 2021

The right of Patrick Bennett to be identified as
the Author of this work has been asserted in
accordance with the Copyrights, Designs and
Patents Act 1988.

ISBN 978 1 3981 0548 5 (print)
ISBN 978 1 3981 0549 2 (ebook)

British Library Cataloguing in Publication Data.
A catalogue record for this book is available from
the British Library.

Typesetting by SJmagic DESIGN SERVICES, India.
Printed in the UK.

Contents

Introduction

Lincolnshire, England's second-largest county, is an area rich in railway history. No fewer than six different pre-Grouping railway companies were represented within its borders. First to arrive on the scene in 1848 was the Midland Railway branch from Nottingham to Lincoln, a line built by the scheming 'Railway King' George Hudson to try to prevent the Great Northern building its line from London to York. The GN's first foray into the county was the 'Loop Line', which ran via Boston to Lincoln. Simultaneously, the East Lincolnshire Railway pushed the line on further to Grimsby via Louth. In the same period the Great Central was busy in the north of the county extending its line from Sheffield to Grimsby, New Holland and Lincoln. The GN 'Towns' route via Grantham followed shortly and both the GN and GC developed further lines in their areas of influence as the century progressed.

In 1882 the Great Northern & Great Eastern Joint Line running northwards through the county was created, to be followed in 1893 by the Midland & Great Northern Joint Line running east–west through the south of the county. The Lancashire, Derbyshire & East Coast Railway was a latecomer on the scene, completing its line to Lincoln just before the end of the century. The early years of the twentieth century saw the construction of two light railways in the north of the county. One of these, the Isle of Axholme Light Railway, was a joint line representing the interests of the Lancashire & Yorkshire Railway and the North Eastern Railway in the county.

As well as the more conventional lines, there were also some more unusual railways. These included the ephemeral Lord Willoughby's Railway; The Alford & Sutton Tramway; the Cranwell branch of the RAF; the potato railways; and not forgetting the Grimsby & Immingham Light Railway in the north-east of the county. Together, they form a fascinatingly diverse railway story.

The photographs by Ben Brooksbank, Geoffrey Skelsey, Lamberhurst and Phil Sangwell are reproduced under the Creative-Commons Attribution Share-alike Licence 2.0. Every attempt has been made to seek permission for copyright material in this book. However, if we have inadvertently used copyright material without permission or acknowledgement we apologise and will make the necessary correction at the first opportunity.

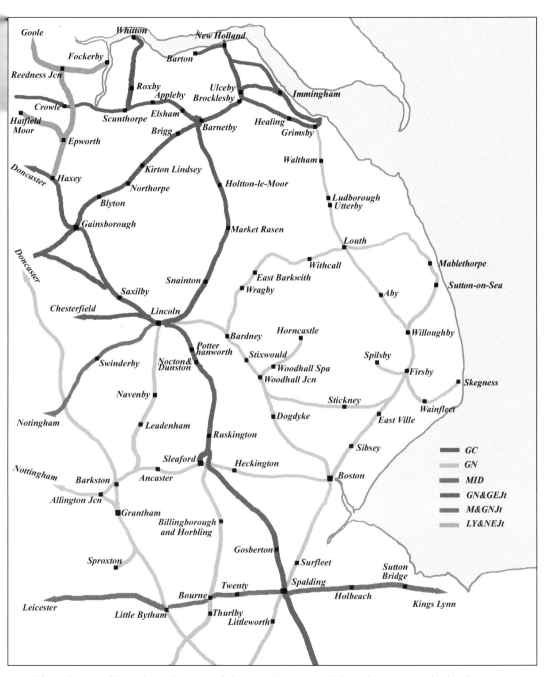

The railways of Lincoln at the time of the 1923 Grouping. Selected stations and other locations are shown.

The Midland at Lincoln

The first railway to penetrate the county of Lincolnshire was the Midland Railway's line from Nottingham to Lincoln. This line was built by George Hudson in an effort to frustrate the attempts of the London & York Railway (later the GNR) to build a line from London to York via Peterborough and Lincoln. Hudson thought an already established line would obviate the need for a second one. Built upon almost entirely level terrain there were few engineering difficulties and the line opened on 4 August 1846. The terminus was at Lincoln St Marks, where in 1985 shortly before closure a Class 120 dmu departs with a service for Nottingham. After closure services were diverted to Lincoln Central. (Lamberhurst)

Many years earlier on 10 November 1923, Johnson Class '1853' 4-2-2 No. 640 waits to depart from St Marks with a service for Nottingham. Introduced in the 1890s, these single-wheelers were all withdrawn by the end of the 1920s.

Apart from the terminus there were just three MR stations in Lincolnshire: Swinderby, Hykeham, and Thorpe on the Hill. The latter closed to passengers in 1955. Hykeham is seen in Midland days. Today it has a basic hourly service provided by East Midland Trains.

At Swinderby on 30 August 1998 Class 47 No. 47739 heads towards Lincoln with a diverted ECML service. The signal box is a Midland type 3b dating from 1901 and retains its original sixteen-lever frame. It is a listed building and continues in use in 2020. Swinderby has a basic two-hourly service with additional trains in the peaks. LNER also runs trains to Lincoln by this route but they do not stop at these two stations.

The Great Central in North Lincolnshire

Grimsby to New Holland and Barton

The Sheffield, Ashton & Manchester Railway, having reached Sheffield in 1848, was looking for an outlet to the east. At the same time, the Sheffield & Lincoln Junction Railway was promoting a route from Sheffield to Gainsborough, while the Great Grimsby & Sheffield Junction Railway was interested in the route on to Grimsby. In 1846 these two companies, together with the Sheffield & Lincolnshire Extension Railway and the Grimsby Docks Company, merged with the SA&M to form the Manchester, Sheffield & Lincolnshire Railway. The GG&SJ station at Grimsby Town survives and is very little altered from this nineteenth-century view.

Grimsby is the only station in North Lincolnshire to retain an overall roof, although this is a modern replacement. The station is seen on 5 September 1989 before resignalling took place.

Right: A view towards Grimsby station from the east as a Class 142 'Pacer' leaves for Cleethorpes. The signal box is Garden Street, an MSL type 2 dating from 1881. It was abolished in 1993 along with the other four signal boxes at Grimsby. The crossing gates have been replaced by barriers. Notice the blast wall around the base of the box, built as an air raid precaution.

Below: The line from Grimsby Town to Grimsby Docks and Pier stations opened on 1 August 1853. The Pier station did not last long, being closed in the 1870s. The Docks station remains open, though now reduced to a single platform. This turn-of-the-century view was taken from the north end of the station.

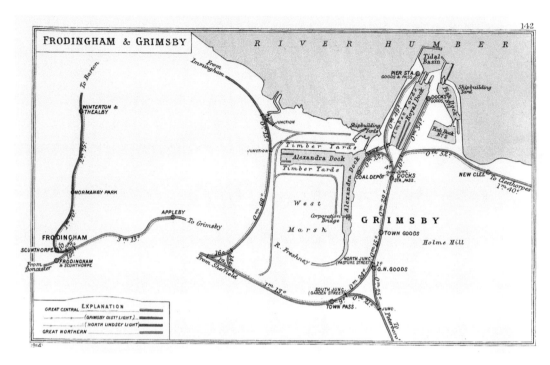

The story of Grimsby Docks was one of continual development by the MSL/GCR. In 1856 the fish dock was opened. A second fish dock was opened in 1879. By 1909 175,000 tons of fish were being landed annually. Nearly all of this left by train. In 1880 the new Alexandra Dock was opened with a connecting line from Great Coates station. Connecting into this line from 1906 was the Grimsby District Light Railway, which served primarily to transport workers from Grimsby to the new docks. The Humber Commercial Railway from Ulceby to the docks at Immingham was opened in 1910 and extended to the Eastern Jetty in 1912. Also in 1910 the Barton & Immingham Light Railway opened between Immingham and Killingholme, extended to Goxhill in 1911. The map shows the situation at Grimsby before the First World War.

Robinson designed a locomotive specifically for the fast fish traffic. This was the Class 8 4-6-0 (LNER Class B5), fourteen of which were built between 1902 and 1904. These were saturated engines but between 1926 and 1936 all were rebuilt with superheated boilers. These locomotives were inevitably known as 'fish engines', one of which, No. 1070, is seen at Leicester in 1910 with a Grimsby to London fish train.

The popularity of Cleethorpes as a seaside destination is evident from this early view. The branch from Grimsby Docks opened as a single track in 1863, followed by doubling in 1874.

The line from Grimsby to New Holland opened on 1 March 1848. Healing was not one of the original stations on the line and did not open until 1 April 1881. A Great Central 4-4-0 arrives with a train for Grimsby in this early twentieth-century view.

An early photograph of Ulceby station. The line from Ulceby to Barton was proposed for closure in the Beeching report. A vigorous local campaign saved the line and today it is supported by the Friends of the Barton Line.

By the time of this 1993 view much had already changed, and since then further changes have taken place. Ulceby South Junction signal box was abolished in 2016 and the crossing gates were replaced by barriers. Note the BR(ER) blue running-in board, now also gone.

Thornton Abbey replaced an earlier temporary station named Thornton Curtis. During the Second World War there was an American base at Goxhill. The servicemen seen here are about to board the 5.15 to Grimsby and Cleethorpes.

The station buildings here at Goxhill are of a standard pattern used by the MSL and found at small stations all over North Lincolnshire. Goxhill retains its signal box, which also controls a manual crossing. It is one of the last in the area and is fringe to York ROC.

New Holland was not the ultimate destination of the MSL. It was merely a means of reaching Hull. The Humber Ferries were authorised in 1846 and a pier constructed for the transhipment of passengers and goods. The opening of the Humber Bridge saw the end of the ferry services. Both New Holland Pier and New Holland Town stations were closed and a new station was built to the south. This view shows Barrow Road Crossing signal box, still active in 2020, with New Holland station on the other side of the crossing gates.

New Holland Pier station in 1976. A dmu stands in the station with a service for Cleethorpes. Notice the coal wagons and tubs used to fuel the ferry steamers. As well as the Town and Pier stations there was a four-road engine shed and extensive sidings alongside the dock. From the earliest days New Holland was the main eastern terminus of the MSL and very busy with traffic for Hull. In 1872 there were forty-five passenger arrivals and departures, as well as twenty goods and coal trains. (Geoffrey Skelsey)

Another view of New Holland Pier, this one taken on 1 July 1972, showing a Class 114 unit standing at the platform. Note the lovely old lower-quadrant signals and their ball-and-spike finials. (Phil Sangwell)

The *Lincoln Castle* was supplied to the LNER in 1940 specifically to work the Humber ferry service, which she did from 1941 to 1978. The British Railways double arrow emblem on the funnel seems to have been wrongly applied.

New Holland to Barton opened on 1 March 1849, with the intermediate halt of Barrow Haven coming into use on 8 April 1850. This is Barton-on-Humber in May 1976. A Class 114 unit waits to leave for Cleethorpes. These units were built specifically for the Lincolnshire and South Humberside area. For a period in 1905/6 a steam railcar was used on the branch. It was not a success. (Geoffrey Skelsey)

Barrow Haven about 1910. Facilities are rudimentary. The signal post has arms for both directions, which appear to be worked from the wooden cabin on the right. Today the facilities are even more rudimentary. Barrow Haven has a service every two hours to Cleethorpes or Barton.

Ulceby to Gainsborough and Lincoln

The line from Ulceby to Brigg opened on 1 November 1848. This is the magnificent Jacobean-style Brocklesby station, disused since its closure in 1993. Its splendour is owed to the fact that it was the home station of the Earl of Yarborough, who lived at Brocklesby Hall and was chairman of the MSL at the time of its construction in 1848. Lord Yarborough and his guests had their own private waiting room in the station. Until 1888 New Holland was the principal destination of the line and passengers for Grimsby had to change here.

Barnetby in the early years of the twentieth century. These are the original buildings. The station was rebuilt when the line was quadrupled through here following the opening of Immingham Docks in 1910. The locomotive arriving to take the gentlemen to work in Grimsby is Class C4 4-4-2 (GCR Class 8B) No. 263, a type introduced by Robinson in 1903. The locomotive on the left is Sacre D12 double-framed 4-4-0 (GCR Class 6B) No. 434B. This locomotive was involved in an accident at Penistone when it broke a crank axle and twenty-four passengers were killed.

On 17 April 1961 O1 2-8-0 No. 63619 approaches Barnetby with a westbound train of empty wagons. (Ben Brooksbank)

Just beyond Barnetby is Wrawby Junction, where the lines from Scunthorpe, Gainsborough and Lincoln meet. Until 2015 the junction was controlled by a 137-lever signal box working a magnificent array of semaphore signals. The three gantries are for the Down goods, the Down slow, and the Down fast. The left-hand signal of each is for the Lincoln line, the centre for the Gainsborough line and the right-hand one for the Scunthorpe line. On 6 September 1989 a Class 150 passes with the 08.58 Newark Northgate to Cleethorpes. On the left is Class 20 No. 20096.

Heading away from Wrawby Junction on the Lincoln line is No. 150120 with the 12.50 Cleethorpes to Newark Northgate. It is passing a typical Great Central gantry. The taller signal is for the Up fast, the lower one for the Up slow. The pair of subsidiary signals are for the reception sidings. The doll on the left was for the signal that controlled entry to the engine shed.

Brigg once had substantial buildings and an overall roof. Even the building shown here has now been demolished and today the platforms are bare apart from a couple of 'bus shelters'. On 16 November 1991 No. 150134 arrives with the 13.45 Sheffield to Cleethorpes to pick up a lone passenger.

To complete the through route from Manchester, the lines from Brigg to Gainsborough, and Gainsborough to Woodhouse Junction were opened on 2 April and 16 July 1849 respectively. The next station east of Brigg was Scawby and Hibaldstow. The locomotive No. 835 was of a design introduced by Parker in 1892. Further examples to the same design were built by Pollitt & Robinson. Scawby station closed in 1968.

Kirton Lime Sidings signal box was built by the Railway Signal Company for the MSL in 1886. Abolished in 2016, it remains as a listed structure. Class 47 No. 47224 passes by with a train of tanks bound for Immingham. In the background is the branch into the quarry, still active at the time of this photograph in August 1989 but now long out of use.

The rather elegant Kirton Lindsey station, seen in 1989. In the left background is the 1,334-yard Kirton Tunnel.

Northorpe station closed to passengers in 1955 and to freight in 1964. Passing the signal box on 19 August 1989 is a Class 110 unit with the 14.29 Cleethorpes to Sheffield.

Blyton station, another MSL station building typical of those in the area. Closure to passengers came in 1959 and to goods in 1964. The buildings, which are listed, remain in private hands.

Gainsborough Central station seen at probably its nadir. Station buildings all gone and a service of just three return services between Cleethorpes and Huddersfield on Saturdays only. In 1995 'Pacer' unit No. 142080 departs with the SO 14.29 Cleethorpes to Huddersfield. Things are better in 2020. There is an hourly weekday service to Sheffield and the Saturdays-only trains to Cleethorpes continue.

Beyond Gainsborough is the bridge over the Trent where the lines from Grimsby and Lincoln meet and then diverge to form the lines to Doncaster and Sheffield. There was originally a signal box at each end of the bridge. On 25 March 1912 a collision occurred between GER and GNR freight trains, which also demolished the Trent East signal box. A new signal box was built to replace both the west and east boxes.

The GG&SJ was initially authorised to build a branch from Barnetby to Market Rasen, later extended to Lincoln. Opening to Market Rasen took place on 1 November 1848, and the line was extended to Lincoln on 18 December. There were originally ten stations on the line. Claxby and Usselby closed in 1960, with the others following in 1965. The sole survivor, Market Rasen, had its overall roof removed in the 1940s and in the early twenty-first century started to fall into dereliction. In 2014 it was sold at auction and, with finance from various sources, restored as a community facility. Here the station is seen in better days with a MS&L Class 2 4-4-0 waiting to depart with a northbound service.

Holton-le-Moor station opened with the line in 1848 and closed in 1965. The signal box is a MS&LR type 3 dating from 1890 and was still active in 2020. The photograph was taken in 1989.

There was never a station at Stainton, only a level crossing box that has now been replaced by automatic barriers. On 6 September 1989 a Class 150 dmu heads over the crossing with a Grimsby–Newark service.

The Great Northern
Loop Line and Its Branches

The Great Northern Railway Act passed on 26 June 1846 authorised a line from London to York via Peterborough, Grantham and Retford. It also authorised the Lincolnshire Loop line, running from Peterborough via Spalding, Boston, Lincoln, Gainsborough and back to the main line at Bawtry. In fact the Loop actually gained access to the GN main line at Retford, using the MSL route. The first section from Peterborough to Lincoln opened on 17 October 1848. Littleworth opened at that time. It closed to passengers on 11 September 1961 and to freight three years later. On 20 June 1991 a Class 108 unit, resplendent in green livery, passes over the level crossing with the 15.31 Sheffield–Peterborough.

Above and below: These two views illustrate how diminished the railway of today is. The first was taken probably at the end of the nineteenth century and the second in July 1989. Once the meeting place of six lines, Spalding is now just a through station on the line from Peterborough to Sleaford. It could have been worse; the line from Peterborough to Spalding closed on 5 October 1970 but reopened on 7 June the following year.

This locomotive started life in 1912 as Robinson 8K No. 1220. Robinson considered the 8K his best design and a total of more than 400 were built, many for the Railway Operating Division during the First World War. Fifty-eight of the class, including No. 63803, were rebuilt by Thomson as Class O1 in the period between 1945 and 1949. Allocated to 31B March in 1960 when this photograph was taken, No. 63803 was withdrawn in March 1963. (Lamberhurst)

The station at Surfleet opened some months after other stations on the Loop line. Being some way from the tiny settlement it purported to serve, the station's main business was agricultural freight. Along with the other stations between Spalding and Boston passenger services were withdrawn in 1961, while freight continued for a few more years. The line itself remained open until October 1970 when it closed along with much of the network in East Lincolnshire.

With the arrival of more modern types on the Great Northern main line the Stirling singles were relegated to secondary duties, as in this scene with 4-2-2 No. 221 heading away southwards from Boston.

Many years later another train prepares to head southward out of Boston. This is the summer Saturdays 12.48 Mablethorpe–Derby Friargate headed by B1 4-6-0 No. 61299. (Ben Brooksbank)

Contrast the scene above with this photograph taken on 15 July 1989 of Class 31 No. 31285 pulling into Boston with a service for Skegness.

This is the entry to Boston Docks seen in 1989. The docks remain rail connected and see regular freight services.

Between Boston and Lincoln the Loop line was built on the east bank of the Witham Navigation, although the original intention was to build on the right bank. The GNR purchased the waterway in 1846 and was responsible for its maintenance. This is Langrick station in about 1910. As elsewhere on the line the station has been built in an Italianate style, but in this case with two rather than three storeys. The station closed to all traffic on 17 June 1963.

At Dogdyke we see the three-storey 'tower' style of building. The stations along the Witham were built near where there was a ferry or bridge to the station. The ferry at Dogdyke was particularly important as the village of Dogdyke was on the opposite bank.

Woodhall Junction was originally named Kirkstead. It was renamed in 1922. At the head of a Lincoln–Boston train is LNER Class D2 4-4-0 No. 2175, an Ivatt design introduced at the turn of the century. On the right is the bay for Horncastle trains. A peculiarity of this arrangement was that trains for Horncastle had to first be propelled out of the station before gaining the Horncastle branch, which left the main line at a north-facing junction. (W.A. Camwell)

The Horncastle branch was opened by the Horncastle & Kirkstead Junction Railway Company on 11 August 1855. The intermediate station at Woodhall Spa was initially little more than a halt. The line was worked from the outset by the GNR but the H&KJR remained independent until the 1923 Grouping. The arrival of the railway led to the rapid development of the spa and the station was rebuilt in 1889. Some time after that date a Stirling 2-4-0 No. 292 stands at the platform with a train from Horncastle.

The branch lost its passenger service on 13 September 1954. Before that there had been a basic service of five trains a day, plus a pick-up freight. The freight traffic, of which livestock was a considerable part, kept the line open until 5 September 1971. In the early post-war years Parker N5 0-6-2T is seen running round its train at Horncastle.

The Kirkstead & Little Steeping Railway was opened by the GNR in 1913 as a shortcut to its seaside resorts. The New Line, as it was always known, ran from Coningsby Junction to Bellwater Junction. Built as a double line it obviated the need for trains bound for the seaside resorts to reverse at Boston or Louth, as had been the case previously. The initial timetable of five trains daily soon reduced to four and by 1947 there were just three trains with an additional service on Saturdays that ran between Lincoln and Coningsby. The regular trains were heavily supplemented by holiday and excursion traffic. The line closed, as did so many others in East Lincolnshire, on 5 October 1970. In the early 1950s B1 4-6-0 No. 61063 heads through Stickney with a special working. (W.A. Camwell)

Stixwould seen from a passing train in 1970, the last year of passenger operations. The station closed to passengers on 5 October. Services were sparse indeed. In 1950 Stixwould had just four trains a day with one on Sundays. These trains ran between Boston and Lincoln. As well as the regular services there were the popular fishermen's specials which ran from Yorkshire to the stations along the Witham. The railway between Boston and Lincoln has been converted into a path and cycle way, named the Water Rail Way. A clever play on words – the water rail is a secretive bird of aquatic habitats. (Lamberhurst)

Bardney opened as Bardney and Wragby on 17 October 1848. It became a junction with the opening of the first section of the Louth & Lincoln Railway on 9 November 1874. It was renamed Bardney in 1881. Passenger services were withdrawn in 1970 but the line to Lincoln remained open until 1980 in order to service the sugar factory at Bardney.

The Louth & Lincoln Railway received its Act on 6 August 1866. The promoters envisaged this new line giving better access to the Midlands from East Lincolnshire. The fact that the junction was at Bardney rather than Five Mile House, which would have given direct access to Lincoln, rather negated this ambition. Another motivation was the large deposits of ironstone along the route of the line, which the company expected to exploit. Wragby was one of the two stations on this single-track line which had a passing loop.

Progress in building the line was slow due to the difficult terrain, which needed the construction of two tunnels: the 557-yard South Willingham tunnel, and the 971-yard Withcall tunnel. Despite these tunnels there were still gradients as steep as 1 in 70. The line was finally opened between Bardney and South Willingham for goods in 1874, and throughout on 28 June 1876. Passenger trains started on the following 1 December. East Barkwith, seen here, was the other station with a passing loop.

On the 22-mile line there were stations at Kingthorpe, Wragby, East Barkwith, South Willingham and Hainton, Donington-on-Bain, Withcall, and Hallington. Around the turn of the century Stirling F2 0-4-2 No. 557A stands at South Willingham with a train for Louth.

At Withcall in 1947 Ivatt C12 4-4-2T No. 7352 stands with a service for Bardney. At this time there were just two trains per day, taking about 45 minutes to complete the journey. There was an extra service on Saturdays. (W.A. Camwell)

Hallington had only one train per day in 1947, and this was by request only. Passenger services on the line were withdrawn on 3 November 1951. Donington to Louth closed to freight traffic in 1956, and the rest of the line closed completely in 1960.

Lincoln

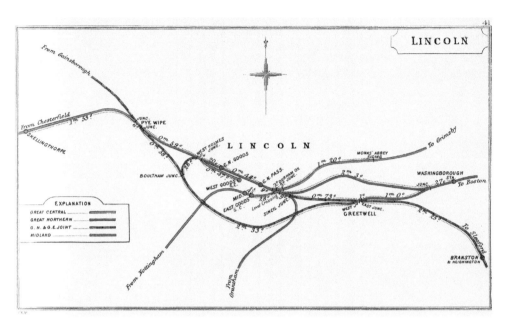

The 1914 Clearing House map of the layout at Lincoln.

Pelham Street crossing, also known as Durham Ox crossing, at the eastern end of Lincoln station caused considerable problems for road traffic until a bridge was built in 1961. All traffic for Grimsby, Sleaford and Boston had to pass this way. The gates also had to be closed for shunting and light engine movements, as seen here. On 21 May 1956 Thomson B1 4-6-0 No. 61326 shunts some wagons. (Ben Brooksbank)

Above: Pelham Street Junction and signal box. On 1 July 1991 a Class 101 unit approaches with the 16.15 Skegness to Doncaster. The tracks on the left are the Grimsby lines. The single track to the left of the train is the Washingborough branch, the remains of the Loop line to Boston.

Right: These are the Grimsby lines on the approach to Pelham Street. A Grimsby–Newark train approaches Lincoln station. The train on the left is waiting to cross over to the Up line in order to change platforms at Lincoln station. The 2007–8 resignalling allowed for reversible running at the Lincoln platforms, meaning this kind of manoeuvre is no longer necessary.

On the same date another Class 101 dmu heads through Holmes Yard with the 15.25 Doncaster to Lincoln. On the right is the GNR locoshed, since demolished and replaced by an events venue named The Engine Shed. The signal box is East Holmes. Also note the typical GNR concrete signal post.

The view from the west end of Lincoln station. High Street signal box is no longer active but has been preserved as it is a listed building. It was built in 1874 and is a GNR type 1 box with a thirty-six-lever frame dating from 1892. The plinthed shunter on the right is D3167. It was purchased by Lincoln City Council in 1988, the year before this photograph was taken. It is now at the Lincolnshire Wolds Railway.

In 1905 there was a typhoid epidemic in Lincoln. Fresh water was brought from Willoughby by rail using old locomotive tenders. Stirling 0-4-2 No.718 is seen with its rake of tenders.

Cattle and sheep in the process of being loaded at Lincoln. Livestock was an important traffic for the railways until supplanted by road transport in the 1960s.

The East Coast Main Line

The Great Northern's 'Towns Line' via Grantham, Newark and Retford opened on 1 August 1852. Stations on the section that ran through Lincolnshire were at Little Bytham, Corby, Great Ponton (south of which was the High Dyke mineral branch), Grantham, Barkston, Hougham, and Claypole. All but Grantham were closed in the mid to late 1950s. This section of line includes the famous 1 in 178/200 Stoke Bank, down which *Mallard* achieved the world speed record for steam on 3 July 1938. In 2020, the passenger train operators seen on this stretch of line are London North Eastern Railway, Hull Trains, East Midland Railway, and Grand Central. There are also a number of freight operators. On 17 May 1962 Thomson L1 2-6-4 No. 67767 waits to depart from Grantham with a service for Derby. (Ben Brooksbank)

Opposite below: A mysterious accident occurred at Grantham on 19 August 1906, which led to fourteen deaths. A mail train headed by Ivatt Atlantic No. 276 was due to call at Grantham. However, instead of stopping, the train ran through the station and derailed on points that were set against it. Both the driver and fireman were killed and the reason the train failed to stop has never been discovered.

Standing at the Up Main platform on 28 March 1956 is B12/3 4-6-0 No. 61580 with the 09.55 to Peterborough North. (Ben Brooksbank)

On 7 March 1896 an accident occurred at little Bytham when a train became derailed, leaving three dead.

Nottingham to Boston

The Ambergate, Nottingham & Boston & Eastern Junction Railway arose out of the merger of three schemes with similar aims. Its Act was passed in 1846 but insufficient funds led only to the section of line from Nottingham (actually Colwick Junction on the MR line to Lincoln) to Grantham. The AN&B&ER station in Grantham was at Old Wharf. The line opened in July 1850. The GNR 'Towns' line station opened two years later, at which point the AN&B&ER station closed and trains then called at the GNR station. The line was worked by the GNR from 1855 and leased from 1861. The AN&B&ER remained an independent company until the Grouping. Grantham GNR station is seen in 1902. Standing at the platform with a northbound service is Ivatt D1 4-4-0 (LNER D2) No. 1376. These engines were often used on services between Grantham and York.

Above: It was left to another company, the Boston, Sleaford and Midland Counties Railway, to complete the line to Boston. Barkston Junction to Sleaford opened on 16 June 1857, and Sleaford to Boston on 13 April 1859. It was worked from the outset by the GNR and absorbed by that company in 1864. There were stations at Honington, Ancaster, Rauceby, Sleaford, Heckington, and Swineshead. Hubberts Bridge opened in 1860. On 4 April 1992 a Class 108 unit forming the 12.48 Skegness to Nottingham approaches Ancaster. Note the disused grain loading siding on the right together with its attendant ground frame.

Right: The line from Allington Junction to Barkston East Junction opened in 1875. This allowed trains to avoid a reversal at Grantham. Allington Junction signal box dates from this time.

Trains travelling from Grantham to the Sleaford line had to run 'wrong line' for a short distance on the ECML before gaining the curve from Barkston South to Barkston East. In 1998 a Class 156 unit can be seen carrying out this manoeuvre. In order to avoid this situation, in 2005 a new curve from Allington East to Allington North Junction was constructed. The old signal box was demolished and a new Allington box opened. At the same time the Barkston South to Barkston East curve was removed.

On 2 June 1989 a Cravens Class 105 unit passes Sleaford East signal box as it enters the station with a Skegness–Doncaster service. At one time Sleaford had North, South, East and West boxes. In 2020, only the West and East boxes survive. The latter dates from 1882 and is a Grade II listed building.

On 19 September 1954 *Trains Illustrated* magazine organised a railtour that started at Liverpool Street, covered parts of Norfolk and Lincolnshire and returned from Grantham to King's Cross behind Peppercorn A1 4-6-2 No. 60136 *Alcazar*. Like many LNER 'Pacifics' a number of A1s were named after famous racehorses. *Alcazar* won the St Leger in 1936. The train is seen at Sleaford. (Ben Brooksbank)

On 10 April 1993 Riddles 4MT 2-6-4T No. 80080 powers through Heckington with the 'Jolly Fisherman' excursion to Skegness. The GNR type 1 signal box dates from 1876. It was still active in 2020. The very typical GNR concrete signal post has now been replaced by one in steel. There is a small museum in the station building.

Honington to Lincoln

The line from Honington to Lincoln opened on 15 April 1867, giving a more direct route to Lincoln for trains from London. There were stations at Caythorpe, Leadenham, Navenby, Harmston and Waddington. Unlike the other stations on the line, Leadenham was built of stone at the insistence of a local landowner. The building survives as a private dwelling.

Navenby along with the other stations on the line, except for Leadenham, lost its passenger service in 1962. The line was not one of those recommended for closure in the Beeching Report. In fact it was recommended that it should be retained as the main route to Lincoln and that the Newark line be closed. This was not to be and the line closed in 1965 with Lincoln trains reverting to the Newark route.

The East Lincolnshire Railway and Its Branches

To the Directors of the East Lincolnshire Railway
This print of the LOUTH RAILWAY STATION is most respectfully dedicated

The East Lincolnshire Railway was authorised by an Act of 26 June 1846 to build a line from Grimsby to Boston. At Grimsby it would connect with the MS&L line from Grimsby to New Holland and at the southern end with the GNR Loop line, thus giving access to London and the south. The GNR leased the line from the outset, with an annual payment to the ELR of £36,000. The station at Louth was designed by Weightman and Hadfield of Sheffield. It is a listed building and survives as residential accommodation.

The section from Louth to Grimsby opened on 1 March 1848 at the same time as the Grimsby – New Holland line. There were stations at Ludborough, North Thoresby, Holton-le-Clay and Waltham. The initial service was of five trains daily. An Ivatt Class C1 4-4-2 arrives at Ludborough station with a southbound service. It closed to passengers on 11 September 1961 and to freight in 1965. Ludborough is the headquarters of the Lincolnshire Wolds Railway.

The GNR had an agreement with the MS&L to run its trains through to New Holland in return for which the MS&L had running powers as far as Louth. This arrangement did not last long as the MS&L was persuaded by other companies, principally the LNW, to cease cooperation with the GNR which it saw as a threat to its London traffic. North Thoresby station is seen from a passing train shortly before closure, which occurred on 5 October 1970 along with the remaining stations on the line. In 2009 the station was reopened as the northern terminus of the preserved Lincolnshire Wolds Railway.

Waltham was originally Waltham and Humberstone. In 1849 the line saw six passenger services on weekdays which had increased to eight by the 1920s. There was a considerable amount of freight traffic, including fast fish trains to London. Waltham closed to passengers on 11 September 1961 and to freight on 15 June 1964.

In December 1905 a number of halts were opened between Louth and Grimsby. These were at Fotherby, Utterby, Grainsby, Holton Village, and Weelsby Road and Hainton Street. These halts were serviced by Ivatt-designed railmotors which were introduced the same year. They were not a great success and all were out of service by 1917. This is Utterby Halt with one of the railmotors in attendance. Trains stopped by request only.

Louth to Firsby opened on 3 September 1848 and Firsby to Boston on 1 October the same year. An early view of Aby station, which was originally called Claythorpe. It became Aby on 1 September 1885. In 1947, the last year of the LNER, Aby just saw three trains per day on weekdays and one on Sundays. It closed to passengers on 11 September 1961.

The original Willoughby station of 1848 was replaced by the second of 1886, seen here. The new station, located to the north of the old one, was built for the opening of the Sutton & Willoughby branch. There were two through platforms and a bay for the branch, which was to the right of the Up platform in this view. In the summer of 1947 Willoughby had a very sparse service of three or four trains a day. However this was boosted on Saturdays when there were through trains from Nottingham, Leicester, Manchester and King's Cross. The station closed along with many others in the area in October 1970.

Firsby station was very similar to Louth. Unlike Louth it did not survive long after the station closed in 1970, being demolished soon after. This is a view looking north from the Up platform taken on 6 June 1968. When the line to Wainfleet opened a third platform was added at the rear of the Up platform. (Lamberhurst)

On the same day, a Class 114 dmu arrives from the south with a service for Cleethorpes. The line on the right with the stationary dmu originally led to the Spilsby branch, while the line curving off to the left was for Skegness. Until the South Curve was completed in 1881 trains for Skegness had to reverse here. Firsby was originally called Firstby. (Lamberhurst)

An Up train approaches East Ville station. Clearly, it has no plans to stop. This was another station that closed to passengers on 11 September 1961. However, the line remains open as it is on the route to Skegness.

Sibsey was once extremely busy with freight traffic, mainly potatoes and beets. During the inter-war years this traffic was dealt with in the eight-road yard, dispatching potato trains daily. Sibsey closed to passengers in 1961 and to freight in 1964. As with East Ville the line itself remains open. The main station building seen in this early view still stands and the signal box remains active.

The Spilsby Branch

The Spilsby & Firsby Railway was authorised in 1865 and opened on 1 May 1868. There was an intermediate station at Halton Holgate. For most of its existence there was a service of eight trains daily but goods traffic was always more important. Passenger services were suspended shortly after the outbreak of the Second World War and never reinstated. The line closed completely in 1958. At the turn of the nineteenth century Spilsby sees the arrival of a train headed by Stirling 0-4-2 No. 122A, rebuilt by Ivatt as Class F3.

The Skegness Branch

The Wainfleet & Firsby Railway was authorised by an Act of 13 May 1869. The single track line was completed by 1871 and saw a service of eight trains daily worked by the GNR. An extension to Skegness followed in 1873. There were stations at Wainfleet, Thorpe Culvert, Croft Bank, later renamed Havenhouse, and Cow Bank, renamed Seacroft and closed in 1953. The Skegness branch was the last place in England to retain GNR somersault signals, as seen here. A Class 101 dmu passes Wainfleet's Down distant with the 11.11 Doncaster to Skegness on 1 July 1991.

Originally, trains coming from the south had to reverse in Firsby station. In order to avoid this, Firsby South curve was added in 1881. This is the line that is still in use. The W&FR was absorbed by the GNR in 1896 and the line was doubled by 1900. The branch currently has a service of fifteen trains daily, though only two of these stop at Thorpe Culvert. The signal box seen in this 1993 photograph has since been demolished and replaced by a new structure. The somersault signals have been replaced by colour lights. On 10 April a Class 153 dmu heads past with a service for Skegness.

Skegness generated considerable holiday and excursion traffic. In 1955 on summer Saturdays Up to forty holiday trains, mainly from the Midlands, would arrive to be accommodated in the twenty-four carriage sidings. On Sunday 24 August 1980 excursion traffic is clearly still buoyant. Lined up ready to depart are, left to right: Class 31 No. 31115; Class 45s Nos 45116, 45049, 45018; and Class 20 No. 20113.

The Mablethorpe Loop

The Mablethorpe loop was 23 miles long and was built over a number of years. The first section from Mablethorpe Junction, about a mile south of Louth, to Mablethorpe was authorised by an Act of 18 July 1872. The line was constructed by the Louth & East Coast Railway and opened on 17 October 1877. The intermediate stations were Grimoldby, Saltfleetby and Theddlethorpe. The L&ECR remained an independent company until bought by the GNR in 1908. This 1960s view shows the crossing and signal box at Mablethorpe Junction. (Lamberhurst)

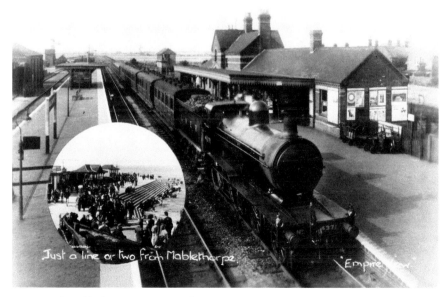

A view of Mablethorpe station in the 1920s. The locomotive is Ivatt Class D2 4-4-0 No. 4371. This long-lived class was introduced at the turn of the century, thirty-one surviving into BR ownership. No. 4371 was not one of these and was withdrawn in 1946.

The popularity of Mablethorpe as a resort can be clearly seen in this photograph taken shortly before the Second World War. Its popularity continued after the conflict and in 1962 Mablethorpe received 402,000 visitors, of whom 110,000 were day trippers and 190,000 holiday makers. All of these visitors would have arrived from the south as the line from Mablethorpe Junction to Mablethorpe closed in 1960.

In this 1960s view Mablethorpe has an air of living on borrowed time, despite the numbers quoted above. As with much of the railway network in East Lincolnshire, the line between Willoughby and Mablethorpe closed on 5 October 1970.

The Sutton & Willoughby Railway opened on 28 July 1884. There was an intermediate station at Mumby Road. This line was built as part of the LD&ECR plans to build a railway from Warrington to the East Coast, in order to export coal. These plans were finally killed off by the development of the docks at Immingham. The three-mile gap between Sutton and Mablethorpe was completed on 14 July 1888. The S&WR was purchased by the GNR in 1902. In the 1960s the driver of a Class 114 dmu surrenders the single line token as it arrives at Sutton. (Lamberhurst)

Stamford–Essendine–Bourne–Lincoln

The town of Stamford is tucked away in the far south-west of Lincolnshire but it was one of the earliest towns in the county to enjoy a train service. Thanks to Hudson's efforts to undermine the Great Northern, the Midland Railway opened its line from Peterborough to Stamford on 2 October 1846. The connection to Leicester opened on 20 March 1848. This elegant station was designed by Sancton Wood.

The Act for the Stamford & Essendine Railway received its assent in 1853 and the line, just under four miles long, opened on 1 November 1856. The Marquess of Exeter, who was the majority shareholder in the S&E, insisted that the station be built in the same Elizabethan style as Burghley House, his seat. There was one intermediate station at Ryhall and Belmesthorpe. The line closed to passengers in 1957 and to goods in 1959. Standing at the platform is one of Patrick Stirling's 0-4-2s, as rebuilt by Ivatt.

G.N. Railway Station, Stamford

The Bourne & Essendine was another line supported by the Marquess of Exeter. The Act was received on 12 August 1857 and the line opened in May 1860. The line was worked from the outset by the GNR, which absorbed the company in 1864. There were two intermediate stations on this seven-mile line, at Thurlby and Braceborough Spa. For most of its life the line had eight trains a day. It closed completely in 1951. A Stirling Class F2 0-4-2 arrives at Thurlby.

A line from Sleaford to Bourne was proposed by the GNR in an effort to thwart the Great Eastern's ambition to build a line through Lincolnshire. Once the Joint line was agreed the line became pointless. However the GNR was obliged to complete the line, which opened in January 1872. The 17½-mile line was single track with a passing place at Bilingborough and Horbling. The other stations were Morton Road, Rippingale, and Aswarby and Sedringham. The line closed to passengers as early as 1930. Freight continued until July 1956 when the section between Bilingborough and Sleaford closed. The surviving section succumbed in 1965. Bilingborough and Horbling is seen in 1961. (Ben Brooksbank)

The station buildings and goods shed seen here at Rippingale station have survived today in remarkably original condition. At one time owned by an enthusiast couple, the station had a length of track on which rested two preserved locomotives.

The Edenham and Little Bytham Railway

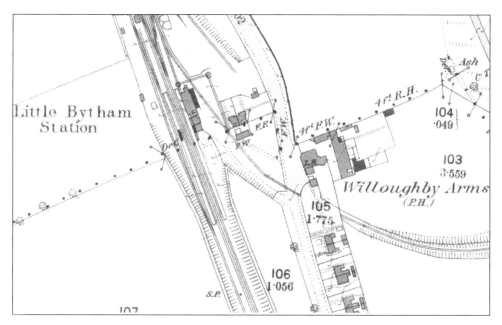

The Edenham & Little Bytham Railway was built by Lord Willoughby de Eresby to connect his country estate at Grimsthorpe with the GNR at Little Bytham. The four-mile line was opened in 1856 and was worked by two 0-4-0 tank engines. Connection was made with the GNR in the goods yard at Little Bytham. By the early 1880s the engines were worn out, passenger services had ceased and freight traffic was being hauled by horses. The line was closed and dismantled soon after.

Further Developments in North Lincolnshire

The South Yorkshire Railway opened a line from Thorne to Keadby in September 1859. There was one intermediate station at Crowle. The railway was constructed for most of its length on the bank of the Stainforth & Keadby Canal, which the company already owned. The proximity of the canal is evident in this view of Crowle station. The line curving off to the left led to Crowle Wharf. In the background can be seen the bridge carrying the Isle of Axholme Joint Railway over the railway and canal, dating this photograph to after 1905.

Further stations were opened soon after completion. One of these, Godnow Bridge to the west of Crowle, did not stay open very long, closing in 1917.

Godnow Bridge signal box seen in 1991. It is interesting to compare this photograph with the previous one. It is clear that the signal box has been rebuilt at some point, losing the central door and the lower windows. This box and the hut were later demolished and a new brick-built box constructed.

The Trent, Ancholme & Grimsby Railway started out as a line to transport iron ore to the River Ancholme. The SYR and MSL became involved and eventually a line from Gunness on the Trent to Wrawby Junction was opened on 1 October 1865. A five-span bridge with a swinging centre section was constructed to carry the railway over the Trent. This opened on 1 May 1866. A new line was built from Keadby Junction to join the bridge and connect with the SYR line. A new station, Keadby and Althorpe, was constructed on the left bank and another, Gunness and Burringham, opposite on the right. The original Keadby station was renamed Keadby for Amcotts and Burringham. It closed in 1874 and became a goods station. This is Keadby Canal junction. The lines to the left lead to the first Keadby station, while those to the right lead to the second – Keadby and Althorpe, now named Althorpe.

This is a view taken from the opposite direction in 2020. The signal box is still there but the lines to the first Keadby station are long gone. The enormous structure in the foreground together with the tracks slides to the left to allow the passage of boats on the canal.

In 1916 a new bridge across the Trent was opened sixty-six yards to the north of the existing bridge. This entailed diverting the lines on each bank to meet the new bridge. The bridge, officially the King George V Bridge, was a 50-metre electrically powered bascule. It also carried a road. The bridge ceased to lift towards the end of the 1950s. On 15 January 2020 a Class 185 TransPennine Express service to Cleethorpes heads onto the bridge.

On the TA&G there were stations at Frodingham (later Scunthorpe), Appleby and Elsham. The first Frodingham station closed in 1886, to be replaced by a new station on a different site named Frodingham and Scunthorpe. The present station was opened in 1928 on yet a further site and named Scunthorpe. On 22 February 2020 a Class 144 'Pacer' waits to depart with the 09.48 to Doncaster.

Scunthorpe was created by the iron and steel industry. For a hundred years, between the first blast furnace starting production and 1964, it was a story of continual expansion. In 2020 steel production at Scunthorpe faces an uncertain future. In this old postcard view of the steel works, note the multiplicity of wagon types and ownership.

Scunthorpe steel works currently has a fleet of Di8 Bo-Bo locomotives originally built for Norwegian Railways. They were later acquired by GB Railfreight. They are powered by a 2,100hp Caterpillar engine and are remotely controlled. Two of these machines are seen at work on 22 February 2020.

Withdrawn locomotives at Scunthorpe. These are Yorkshire Engine Company 'Janus' 0-6-0s.

The Appleby Frodingham Railway Preservation Society offers brake van rides round the extensive rail network at Scunthorpe steel works. On 22 February 2020 one of their engines, Avonside No. 3 *Cranford*, stands at the head of a train of brake vans.

The depot of the AFRPS. The society has a number of locomotives including this PKP 0-6-0T No. 3138 *Hutnik*, currently awaiting restoration.

Appleby station closed in 1967. On 28 June 1990 unit No. 158756 is in charge of the 13.26 Cleethorpes to Manchester.

Elsham lasted somewhat longer, only closing on 3 October 1993. On 28 June 1993 Class 60 No. 60003 heads through with a train of iron ore for Scunthorpe. Appleby and Elsham signal boxes were both built by the Railway Signal Company in 1885. Both are listed, though now abolished.

The Great Northern &
Great Eastern Joint Line

For a long time the GER had wished to penetrate GNR territory, not least to participate in the lucrative Yorkshire coal traffic. Finally, in 1879 an agreement was reached to operate a joint line from Huntingdon to Doncaster, via March and Lincoln. The new joint line incorporated sections of railway that had already been built. These were: Huntingdon to March, built by the ECR/EAR in 1847/51, and the GNR lines from Spalding to March (1867), Pyewipe Junction to Gainsborough (1849), and Gainsborough to Doncaster (1867). The new section of railway needed to complete the line, from Spalding to Pyewipe Junction, was opened on August 1882, at which time the joint committee took over the management of the line. Nocton and Dunston was one of the stations on the new section of line. All were built in a similar style.

Blankney and Metheringham station also opened with the new section of the Joint line. It closed in 1961 but was reopened in 1975 as Metheringham. The signal box retained the name Blankney. It is a rare GNR type 4 box, despite actually being built by the LNER. For this reason and its largely original condition it is a listed building. It lost its status as a block post in 2014 but has been retained to work the crossing barriers, which have now replaced the gates seen in this 1989 photograph.

Pinchbeck was among a whole raft of station closures on the Joint line that took place in 1961. Seen heading through the station in the early years of the twentieth century is a Holden Great Eastern Class F48 0-6-0 (LNER J16) with an Up mineral train.

Gosberton was one of the new stations that came into being when the stretch of line between Spalding and Pyewipe Junction opened in 1882. It closed to passengers on 11 September 1961 and to freight on 5 October 1964. On 20 June 1991 Class 47 No. 47332 approaches Gosberton 100 crossing with a short engineering train. The closed station buildings can be seen to the left of the locomotive. In the background is Gosberton signal box. This signal box was closed and replaced by a new modular box at Gosberton 100 crossing. This too has now closed and the line here is now controlled from Lincoln SCC.

Of the original thirty-three stations on the Joint line just seven remain open. There were numerous signal boxes; in 1988 there were still twenty but today just three control the line. Following the closure of the March–Spalding section of the line in 1982 trains are now routed to/from Peterborough. Potterhanworth, one of the now closed signal boxes, is seen in 1989. The box was a GNR type 1 and dated from 1883.

A staff photograph taken at Ruskington. Interesting that even some of the permanent way staff are wearing ties and no man is without a hat. Ruskington closed in 1961 but reopened along with Metheringham in 1975.

Gainsborough Lea Road was opened by the GNR in 1867. It came under the management of the Joint committee in 1882. This view dates from the early twentieth century.

This is the oil terminal in the goods yard at Gainsborough Lea Road, sadly now closed. It was in fact a loading terminal for oil from the Gainsborough oil field. The Gainsborough field still produces oil but now it is transported by road. The photograph was taken on 29 August 1998.

Between 2012 and 2015 a major upgrade of the Joint line was carried out. The purpose of this was to raise the line speed from 60 to 75 mph and increase the loading gauge to W10 in order to allow the line to be used as a diversionary route by intermodal trains. In the event, the loading gauge was increased to W12. The work involved the closure of thirteen manual signal boxes, upgrade of more than sixty level crossings, relaying of track, and the replacement of numerous bridges. The Sleaford avoiding line was rebuilt to double track. The Joint line is also used as a diversionary route for passenger trains. On 30 August 1998 Class 47 No. 47770 passes through Saxilby with a diverted southbound service.

Haxey and Epworth station. Just to the north of the goods shed seen in the background was a connection with the Axholme Joint line. Haxey and Epworth closed to passengers in 1959 and to goods traffic in 1964.

The Haxey goods shed can be recognised from the previous photograph. On 19 August 1989 a Metro-Cammell Class 101 dmu passes the goods shed at Haxey with a Doncaster–Sleaford service.

The Midland &
Great Northern Joint Line

The Norwich & Spalding Railway opened the line from Holbeach to Sutton Bridge on 1 July 1862. The station seen here replaced an earlier one further south and was opened on 1 March 1866. It became a junction with the arrival of the line from Peterborough and Wisbech on 1 August the same year.

The Crosskeys swing bridge was the third to be built across the Nene. It was completed in 1897 at a cost of £80,000. It was a combined road and rail bridge. It is still in use today as a road bridge. The bell on the signal box was rung when the bridge was about to be opened for river traffic.

Sutton Bridge   The Swing Bridge from Station

The Midland & Great Northern Joint Railway, which came into being in 1893, was the successor to the Eastern and Midlands Railway, itself an amalgamation of a number of smaller companies, including the N&S and the Spalding and Bourne. This is Long Sutton, the next station west of Sutton Bridge. Notice the mixture of upper and lower quadrant signals.

A colourised photograph of Gedney station, just one and a half miles west of Long Sutton and, as was the case with so many of the M&GN stations, situated a long way from the hamlet it purported to serve. In the 1860s and 1870s the E&M was actually known as the Bourn & Lynn Railway.

The N&SR opened its line from Spalding to Holbeach on 15 November 1858. The company ran into financial difficulties and it was to be another four years before the line on to Sutton Bridge was completed. The line here was single track but Holbeach became a crossing place in 1891. The locomotive at the head of the train is a Beyer Peacock 4-4-0 dating from the 1880s.

The extensive goods yard at Moulton indicates the importance of this traffic at these country stations. In fact, after closure to passengers in 1959 this section of railway remained open for goods trains for a further six years, finally succumbing on 1 May 1965.

This is Clay Lake crossing and signal box. Notice the colour light signals with a splitting distant. Clay Lake was the next box from Welland Junction and start of the single-line section to Sutton Bridge. When Clay Lake cleared, the top head would show green, but the distant signals below would both light up and show yellow. When Welland Junction cleared, the distant signal for the route to the right or left would clear to green.

The bridge over the Welland to the east of Spalding. West of here was Welland Bank Junction, the starting point of the avoiding line to Cuckoo Junction, which was completed in May 1893. The bridge over the Welland dates from that time.

Until the Spalding avoiding line opened, all M&GN trains had to call at Spalding and effect a reversal. Seen here some time after 1906 is one of the Johnson 4-4-0s introduced in 1894. These engines were the main express passenger motive power until the takeover by the LNER in 1936.

Counter Drain was opened by the Spalding & Bourne Railway on 1 August 1866. Like so many stations on the M&GN it was nowhere near a settlement so it was named after the nearest physical feature – a drain! It closed briefly between October 1880 and February 1881. It closed to passengers in 1959 but remained open for freight until 1964.

Another station named after a drain, Twenty, also opened with the line on 1 August 1866. In 1893 the line between Bourne and Twenty was doubled, giving the station a second platform and a signal box. Twenty also closed to passengers in 1959 but remained open for freight until 30 March 1964. Notice the token catcher on the left.

At Bourne the M&GN met the GNR line to Lincoln and the Bourne & Essendine line. The latter company acquired a house dating back to 1605 to accommodate the booking office and stationmaster. This was Red Hall, which still stands. This view shows Bourne East signal box and crossing.

The M&GN met the Midland Railway at Little Bytham. The line from Wymondham Junction, just east of Saxby, to Little Bytham was opened on 1 May 1894. There were stations at Edmondthorpe and Wymondham, South Witham, and Castle Bytham. The line between Saxby and Bourne was opened in 1893, providing a much shorter route to the Midlands. The line was MR property as far as Little Bytham and thence to Bourne part of the M&GN. At South Witham alongside the station a limestone quarry was opened in 1907. The hoist which can be seen in the background was used to load the limestone into the railway wagons. South Witham closed with the rest of the system on 28 February 1959.

The Lancashire, Derby & East Coast Railway

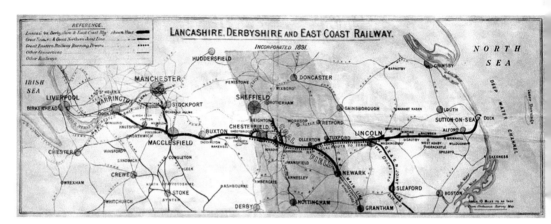

Fifty-one years after the first railway reached Lincolnshire the last to do so arrived. This was the Lancashire, Derbyshire & East Coast Railway, which received its Act on 5 August 1891. It planned to build a line from Warrington to Sutton-on-Sea, where a new dock would be built. The railway was supported by the Derbyshire coal owners who saw the railway as facilitating the export of their coal through the new dock. The railway was also supported by the Great Eastern Railway, which had long craved access to the coalfields. In return for its support it was given running rights as far as Chesterfield.

Opposite above: The railway was unable to raise sufficient funds and only the section between Chesterfield and Lincoln, together with the branch to Beighton, was ever built. This opened in December 1896. The docks at Sutton never materialised. There was only one station in Lincolnshire, at Skellingthorpe. Doddington and Harby was just over the border in Nottinghamshire.

The LD&CR locomotive fleet consisted entirely of tanks, and all were built by Kitson & Company. No. 10 was one of four locomotives of Class B, numbered 9-12 ordered in 1895. They were primarily intended for shunting work. The last of the class was withdrawn in 1948. The company became part of the GCR in 1907 and then at the Grouping part of the LNER. Passenger services, which had in any case been of minimal importance, were withdrawn in September 1955. In 1980 the line was severed at Clifton-on Trent but trains continued to run to High Marnham power station until 2003. The line continues in use as a test track for Network Rail.

Light Railways in North Lincolnshire

The Isle of Axholme Light Railway

The Goole & Marshland Light Railway was authorised in 1898 to build a line from Marshland Junction, on the Doncaster–Goole line, to Adlingfleet via Easton, with branches to Swinefleet and Luddington. In the following year the Isle of Axholme Light Railway was authorised to build a line from Haxey, where it would connect with the GN&GEJt, to Reedness Junction, where it would connect with the G&MLR. Construction was under way when both lines were purchased jointly by the NER and the L&Y, becoming the Isle of Axholme Joint Railway. The photograph shows the opening ceremony on 2 January 1905. The Manning Wardle tank was one of the contractors' locomotives. Halkon was the name of the chairman of the G&MLR.

This is Reedness Junction. The line to the left is the Fockerby Branch and that to the right is the 'main line' to Haxey Junction. On the moors near here and also on Hatfield Moor were 3-foot gauge railway systems for transporting peat, which was later moved by the IAJR. There is currently a project under way, the Crowle Peatland Railway, to restore a number of diesel locomotives and wagons once used on these systems and also lay a demonstration line.

Fockerby was the terminus of the branch from Reedness Junction. It was originally named Garthorpe. On the branch there were stations at Eastoft and Luddington. The line never did reach Adlingsfleet. In pre-Grouping days an L&Y 0-6-0T, train and crew stand at Fockerby having their picture taken.

Crowle Town looking north. There was a service of three trains daily between Haxey and Goole. Passenger services ceased in 1933. More important was goods traffic, which consisted principally of agricultural produce, as well as peat. Notice how busy the goods yard is.

Trains were worked by the L&Y, mainly with Barton Wright 0-6-2Ts and Aspinall 0-6-0s and 2-4-2Ts. One of the 0-6-2Ts is seen at Haxey Junction. These engines, introduced in 1880, were the first of that wheel arrangement in Britain. The LMS introduced a Sentinel rail car in 1926 and a larger one in 1930, which saw out the remaining years of the passenger service.

One of the major features of the railway was Crowle Swing bridge constructed at a cost of £20,000 by the Cleveland Bridge & Engineering Company Limited. The 102-foot bridge was worked by a Crossley oil engine. The bridge was dismantled but the engine has been saved. In this view of the bridge in the 1960s, a Class 47 diesel is heading along the Thorne–Wrawby Junction line.

Another feature of the line is this viaduct crossing Folly Foot and South Engine drains.

Haxey Town station, originally named Haxey Central. The latter title was probably justified as the IALR station was considerably closer to the village than the GCR station of Haxey and Epworth. On the IALR to the north of Epworth the Hatfield goods line branched off. This was not completed until 1909. There were goods stations at Sandtoft and Hatfield Moors.

A view of both Haxey Junction and Haxey and Epworth stations. Haxey Junction is on the left. There was in fact another line joining Haxey. This was the freight only line from Bawtry on the Great Northern main line. This line was very long in gestation, having first been proposed in 1846. It was not finally built until 1912 and was never very much more than a freight siding.

The North Lindsey Light Railway

The North Lindsey Light Railway was a project of the GCR, the intention of which was to join Scunthorpe with the Humber and also service the mines and blast furnaces at Normanby Park. The six miles from Dawes Lane, the NLLR station at Scunthorpe, to Winterton and Thealby and West Halton were opened on 3 September 1906. Winterton and Thealby station is seen in the 1960s on the occasion of a special train, long after closure to passengers. (Lamberhurst)

Winteringham was reached on 13 July 1907 and Whitton on 1 December 1910. Thus following the Act in 1900 it had taken ten years to complete these eleven miles! The initial passenger service of three return trains daily soon declined to one each to Winterton and Whitton and stopped completely in 1925. Whitton station is seen in its early days.

The line north of West Halton closed in 1951 and to Winterton in 1964. It remains open as far as the landfill site at Roxby and at Dragonby there are a number of sidings. There is also the branch to Flixborough Wharf. At Dragonby on 28 June 1993 RFS Industries No. 1 *Terence* shunts a train of steel bar.

Lincolnshire's Other Railways

The Grimsby & Immingham Electric Railway

The GCR opened the Grimsby & District Light Railway between Grimsby and Immingham on 3 January 1910. A steam railmotor provided a service of four trains a day. This service was withdrawn when the GCR opened the G&IER on 15 May 1912. This was a six-mile line that ran from Corporation Bridge to Immingham Town. It was single track with fourteen passing places, some of which were later removed. A double-track extension to the docks was added on 17 November 1913. This involved a reversal at Immingham Town. A further extension to Immingham village was completed in 1915 but was little used. The GDLR survives today as a freight-only line. A line-up of trams is seen at the Immingham terminus on 27 May 1958. (Ben Brooksbank)

Twelve trams for the line were built by Brush and four by the GCR. At 43 feet 8 inches and with seventy-two seats, these were the longest trams in Britain. In 1948 three further cars were purchased from Newcastle Corporation and in 1951 eighteen followed from the Gateshead Tramway. The two types of car can be compared here, with the Gateshead type on the left and the original Brush car on the right.

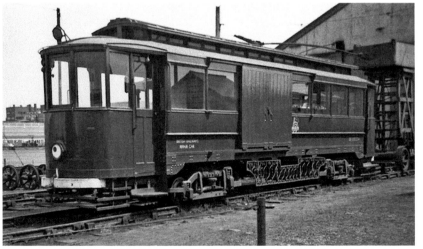

Gateshead car No. 17 was rebuilt by BR as a works vehicle, numbered DE320224. It is seen outside the depot together with the tower vehicle used for maintaining the overhead catenary. (Geoffrey Skelsey)

Car No. 15 is seen passing Cleveland Bridge Works, the tram depot more informally known as Pyewipe. The line was closed from Corporation Bridge to this point on 1 July 1956, making the line considerably less useful. The remainder closed on 1 July 1961. (Geoffrey Skelsey)

The Alford & Sutton Tramway

The A&ST was the conception of Mr B. Dick. The Act was received on 12 August 1880 and construction was completed for the opening on 2 April 1884. The 8-mile line was built to a gauge of 2 feet 6 inches and was constructed along the roadside via Bilsby and Markby, terminating in Sutton-on-Sea at the Jolly Bacchus Inn. There were three 0-4-0 locomotives constructed by three different manufacturers: Black Hawthorn & Co, Merryweather, and Dick Kerr. The first day did not go too well due to the large number of passengers wanting to travel. The last tram did not return from Sutton until midnight. The line proved popular until the completion of the Willoughby–Sutton railway, with which it could not compete. The last trams ran in December 1889.

The Potato Railways

The poor ground conditions, especially in winter, led to a number of farming concerns in Lincolnshire laying down narrow-gauge railway systems. These were the famous potato railways. The two main systems were the Fleet Light Railway near Holbeach and the Nocton Estate system. The Fleet system was built around 1910 to a gauge of 1 feet 11½ inches and extended to some thirteen miles. The Nocton system utilised redundant materials from the trench railways of the First World War. Simplex locomotives provided the motive power. At its most extensive there were thirty miles of track. The main customer for the potato crop was Smith's crisps. Improved roads led to the gradual run down of the system, which finally closed in 1969. Some of the material was reused by the Lincolnshire Coast Light Railway.

RAF Cranwell

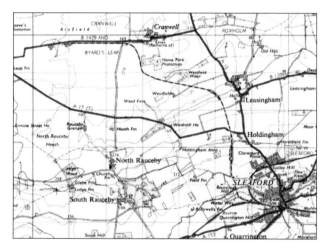

A Royal Naval Air Service station was set up at Cranwell in 1915, later to become RAF Cranwell. A contractor's railway was laid down in 1915/6 to carry materials to the site and it was decided to construct a permanent railway. This was built by the GNR and opened in 1917, though not fully completed until February 1919. The 5.2-mile branch left the Sleaford–Barkston line just west of Sleaford West Junction. There were gradients as steep as 1 in 50. Passenger services were run and there were stations at Slea River, Cranwell and East Camp. This service ceased in 1926 but the line continued to carry freight and on occasion special passenger trains were run. The branch closed completely in 1956 and was lifted the following year.

Locomotive Depots

There were fourteen locomotive sheds and depots in Lincolnshire at one time or another. Pre-Grouping companies represented were Great Central, Great Northern, Great Eastern, Midland, and Midland & Great Northern. The latter company had a two road shed at Spalding at St John's Road. This photograph dates from 1934. The shed closed on 5 March 1960.

The M&GN loco shed at Bourne. Standing outside is one of the Ivatt-designed 0-6-0s acquired by the company in 1900. One of this class was the last of the M&GN engines to be withdrawn, lasting until 1951 and even acquiring a BR number, the only M&GN loco to do so. The shed closed in 1953. In BR days both Bourne and Spalding were sub-sheds of 35A New England.

The Great Eastern had a loco shed at Pyewipe Junction, Lincoln. This was used by engines on the GN&GEJt line. The shed dated from 1907/8 and closed on 2 October 1924. However it continued to be used for watering and crew changing until the 1960s. Lincoln St Marks was the MR shed, situated to the east of Pelham Street crossing. It opened in 1867 and closed in January 1959. There were Great Central sheds at Lincoln, closed in May 1939 but used as a stabling point until 1957; New Holland, a four-road shed opened 1847, closed 1941; and Grimsby, from 1912 a sub-shed of Immingham. The shed at Frodingham was opened by the LNER in 1932 and closed in 1966. The main Great Central shed was at Immingham. Robinson designed the Class 5A 0-6-0T (LNER Class J63) specifically for shunting at Immingham Docks. No. 8208 is seen at Immingham Depot on 21 September 1947. (Ben Brooksbank)

Also seen at Immingham on the same date is ex-GN Class D3 4-4-0 No. 2138. One year short of its half century, No. 2138 has been withdrawn from service and awaits its fate in the scrapyard. (Ben Brooksbank)

The Great Northern had sheds at 40A Lincoln; 40F Boston, a nine-road shed opened 1851, closed 1964; 40C Louth; Stamford East, a sub-shed of New England; Sleaford, a sub-shed of Boston; and Spalding, a sub-shed of New England. The abandoned 40A Lincoln is seen in July 1991. The loco plinthed outside the shed is the unique Ruston & Hornsby diesel-electric departmental shunter No. 97560, which now resides at the Lincolnshire Wolds Railway. The signal box is East Holmes, now out of use but still extant as it is a listed building, being the second-oldest surviving GNR box.

At Lincoln on 13 April 1947 stands Robinson B7 4-6-0 No.1391. This class of four-cylinder mixed traffic engine was introduced in 1921. No. 1391 would last just another three years before being withdrawn. (Ben Brooksbank)

Also at Lincoln on the same date, Great Central Class 8B (LNER Class C4) 4-4-2 No. 2903 waits for its next turn of duty. These handsome locomotives known as 'Jersey Lilies' were introduced by Robinson in the early years of the century. Twenty came into BR ownership but none survived long enough to carry its BR number. (Ben Brooksbank)

At 40C Louth in June 1947 Ivatt C12 4-4-2 No. 7359 waits for its next duty, while a member of staff cleans a carriage the old-fashioned way. (W.A. Camwell)

Grantham loco shed was an important changeover point for engines on the East Coast main line. In January 1957 it had an allocation of fifty-three locomotives, twenty of them Pacifics. Some years earlier, on 13 April 1947, Gresley J39 0-6-0 No. 4965 is seen at the depot. (Ben Brooksbank)